SEE?

FARM

Copyright © **ticktock Entertainment Ltd 2006**
First published in Great Britain in 2006 by ticktock Media Ltd.,
Unit 2, Orchard Business Centre, North Farm Road, Tunbridge Wells, Kent TN2 3XF

ISBN 1 86007 851 6
Printed in China

Picture credits
t=top, b=bottom, c=centre, l=left, r=right
Alamy: 4-5. FLPA: 4-5, 6-7c, 10-11c, 13c, 14cl, 17c, 19c, 20c.
Every effort has been made to trace the copyright holders, and we apologise in advance for any unintentional omissions.
We would be pleased to insert the appropriate acknowledgements in any subsequent edition of this publication.

A CIP catalogue record for this book is available from the British Library.

contents

on the Farm

There is so much to see on the farm – from horses, cows, pigs and other animals to the farmer and the **machinery** that helps him as he works.

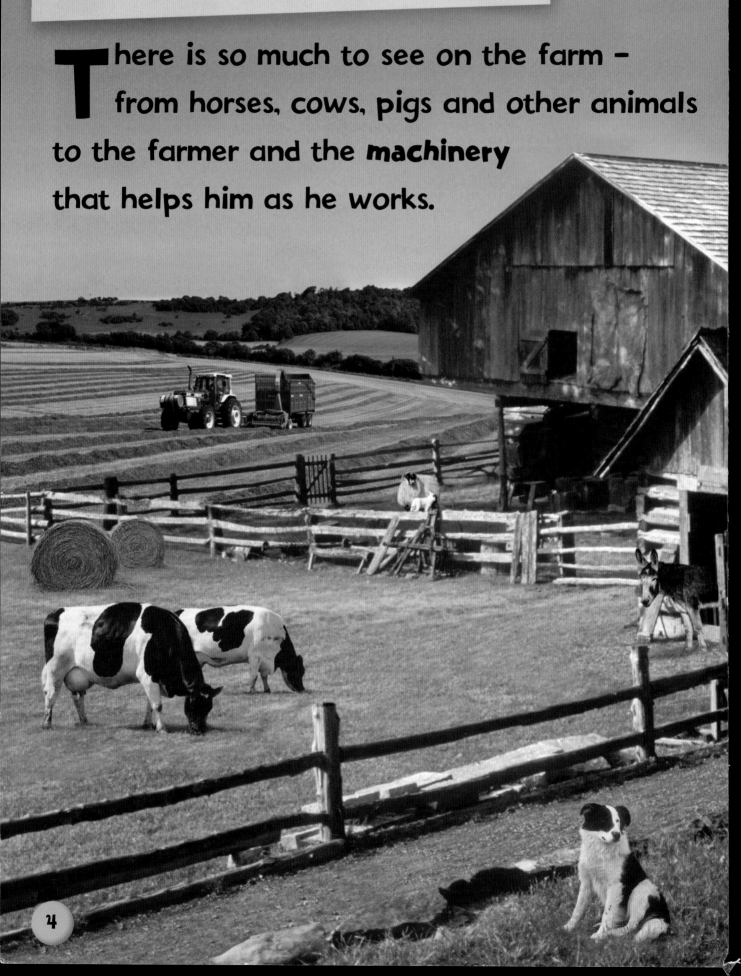

What can you see on the farm?

Horse

Hay bales

Cow

Cockerel

Duck

Sheep

Tractor

Sheepdog

Donkey

Horse

Horses live on a lot of farms. They are used to **herd** animals and for doing heavy work on a farm. Farmers also use horses for riding and racing.

A female horse is called a mare and a baby horse a **foal**. A male horse is called a stallion.

Horses like to eat juicy grass, hay and other plants.

Horses have hooved feet. Some are fitted with metal shoes to protect them from **damage**.

Shire horses are very tall, strong animals with white, fluffy feet. In the past they were used to **plough** fields.

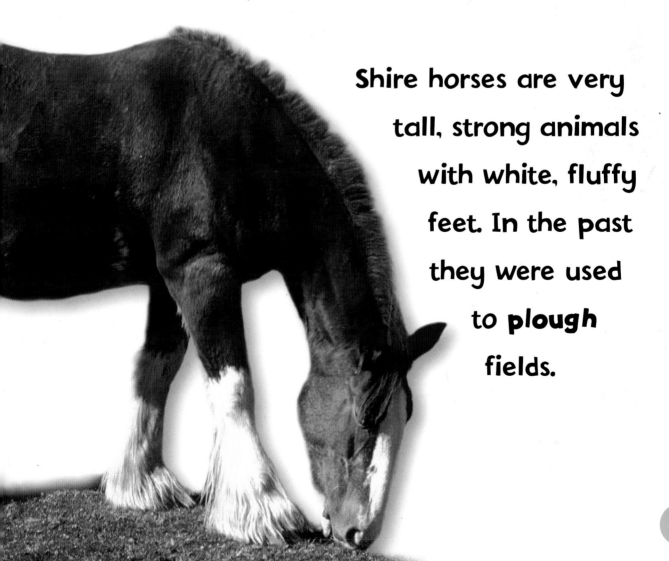

Hay is made from dried grass. Farmers use hay to feed their animals during the winter, when there is no fresh grass.

The hay is made into bundles called bales. These are easier for the farmer to carry.

The bales of hay are piled up to make a **haystack**. This is like a food store for animals.

When the grass is ready in late summer, machines mow it down. This is called harvesting. Then the grass is spread out to dry in the sun to make hay.

Cows live together in a herd. Cows kept to give milk live on dairy farms.

A farmer may keep just a few cows on his farm, or a **herd** of dozens.

Milk comes from a female cow's **udders**, which are underneath her tummy.

Cows can drink about a bathtub full of water a day.

Cows eat grass in the summer. In the winter, cows are fed on hay, which is dried grass.

A cockerel is a male chicken. He wakes up when the sun comes up and makes a sound like "cock-a-doodle-doo".

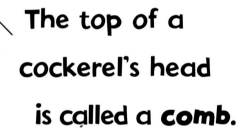

The top of a cockerel's head is called a **comb**.

Cockerels look after all the female chickens on the farm.

Cockerels make a loud sound called a "crow". This screech is a way of marking their territory.

DUCKS

A duck is a bird that likes to live on water. Ducks have **webbed** feet, which help them to swim. They like to live on farmyard ponds.

Ducks make their nests near water. They lay up to 12 eggs, which **hatch** into ducklings.

Baby ducks (ducklings) learn how to swim by copying their parents.

Ducks can only fly for part of the year. Their flight feathers fall out every July. They hide in reeds for about six weeks until they have grown back.

Sheep

Sheep have been kept by farmers for thousands of years. They are best known for their coats of thick, shaggy, soft wool.

Every year, the farmer cuts off (shears) a sheep's wool. It is sent away to make jumpers and rugs.

A female sheep is called a **ewe**. Baby sheep are called lambs.

Lambs are born in the springtime.

They drink their mother's milk.

A ewe with her lamb

 **tractor**

Most farmers use tractors to help them with their work. They are useful because they can pull heavy loads.

Tractors have big, strong wheels that stop them getting stuck in soft ground.

Farmers use tractors for tasks such as making hay or gathering **crops**.

Tractors are used to pull many different machines, such as this **harvester.**

**Tractors can
pull heavy loads**

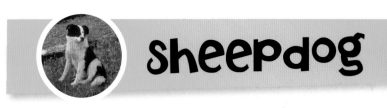

Sheepdog

A sheepdog's job is to round up sheep. Farmers train sheepdogs to understand special whistles, telling them what to do.

Sheepdogs are a special breed of dog called a border collie. They are intelligent and **obedient.**

Farmers teach sheepdogs to round up sheep and **herd** them into pens.

Sheepdogs herd sheep by crouching down low and **stalking** the flock, without taking their eyes off them.

Donkey

Donkeys are members of the horse family. They are strong, but gentle with many uses.

Farmers use donkeys to carry loads, to **protect** sheep and as friends for nervous horses.

Donkeys have long ears and short, stiff **manes**. Their tails end in a tuft of hair.

Donkeys have very **distinctive** voices! They make a rasping noise that sounds like "hee-haw".

Glossary

Comb A large red crest on the top of a cockerel's head

Crop Plants that are grown for food or to make things

Damage Harm or injury to someone or something

Distinctive Easy to recognize

Ewe A female sheep

Foal A young horse

Harvester A farm machine which cuts down crops when they are ready to be harvested

Hatch Break out of an egg

Haystack Bales of hay that are piled up for storage

Herd A group of animals

Machinery Equipment that can do work that used to be done by people

Mane Hair that grows on the head and neck of a horse, donkey or similar animal

Obedient Following orders, commands or instructions

Plough A machine that is used to turn over the ground ready for planting crops

Protect To keep safe from harm

Stalking To follow with the aim of hurting or killing

Udders Part of a cow, where the milk comes out

Webbed Joined together with skin, like a duck's toes or a frog's feet